TIME FOR KIDS READERS

FREEDOM QUILTS

by Carolyn Jackson

Harcourt

Orlando   Austin   Chicago   New York   Toronto   London   San Diego

Visit *The Learning Site!*
www.harcourtschool.com

Making quilts has been a family tradition for people in many parts of the United States.

A Love of Quilts

When she was a girl in Callison, South Carolina, Ozella McDaniel would sit with her family under a big oak tree. The day's farmwork would be done. In the fading light Ozella's mother and grandmother would tell stories to the children.

While they talked, they would mend the family's clothes. They mended the old quilts that warmed their beds. Sometimes they made new ones. Ozella loved to hear stories about the quilts. Once in a while her mother or grandmother would hold up a piece of a quilt to make a point. Ozella also loved the sound of her mother's and grandmother's voices. They made her feel safe and loved. All through her life Ozella would remember those happy times.

When Ozella grew up, she left tiny Callison to go to college. After graduation she continued her studies at Howard University in Washington, D.C. She taught school in California and got married.

TFK DID YOU KNOW

How to Make a Quilt

Plain or fancy, all quilts are made the same way. There are three layers.

1. The top layer can be plain. It can also be made of pieces of cloth arranged in patterns. Some quilt makers just stitch in a design.
2. The middle layer is like the filling in a sandwich. It might be cotton or wool. It might be an old blanket, or even an old quilt. This gives the quilt its warmth.
3. The back of the quilt, the lining, is usually plain. In fancy quilts the lining might be silk. But in early America most quilt backs were made of sturdy cotton.

Once the layers were stacked up, quilters sewed them together. Sometimes they used tiny, almost invisible, stitches. On plain quilts, the layers might just be knotted together at regular spaces with twine.

Mrs. Ozella McDaniel Williams shows one of her quilts.

Many years later she returned to South Carolina. People called her by her married name, Mrs. Ozella McDaniel Williams, or simply Mrs. Williams.

Mrs. Williams wanted to share her love of quilts with others. She began making and selling quilts in a market in Charleston, South Carolina.

Mrs. Williams was proud and well-educated. She knew a lot about her people's past. She would often use that knowledge to grab a customer's attention. "Did you know," she would ask, "that quilts were used by slaves to communicate on the Underground Railroad?" These quilts became known as freedom quilts.

"The Underground Railroad?" many would say. "What's that?"

Here is what she told them. The Underground Railroad wasn't a real railroad. No, it was a web of routes that slaves followed as they walked to their freedom.

The story of slavery in America started in 1619, when English settlers brought Africans against their will to Jamestown, Virginia. In time, slavery became legal in all 13 British colonies.

The colonies became states, and one by one most of the Northern states outlawed slavery. But it remained legal in the South. Some states that bordered the South also permitted it.

Canada outlawed the purchase of new slaves in 1793. The United States had different ideas. It strengthened the rights of slave owners. The U.S. Congress made it a crime for anyone in the United States to protect people trying to escape enslavement. This included the North, where slavery was against the law. And from the very beginning of slavery in the United States, slaves naturally attempted to escape to freedom.

TFK DID YOU KNOW

Africans in Canada

In Canada, formerly enslaved people founded several communities. One of the most successful was the Elgin Settlement in North Buxton, Ontario. The population ranged from 1,200 to 2,000 people. Most people were farmers. Others worked in a sawmill and grist mill, a brickyard, a hotel, a blacksmith shop, a dry goods store, and a few small factories. They also built three churches and a school.

Some residents of Buxton returned to the United States when the Civil War ended. But many stayed behind. Today the community is so small, some people worry that it may not survive. Visitors to Buxton today can visit the Buxton National History Site and Museum.

In 1910, the children and teachers of a school in Buxton proudly pose for a class photo. The school was founded by enslaved Africans who had fled plantations in the United States and went to Canada.

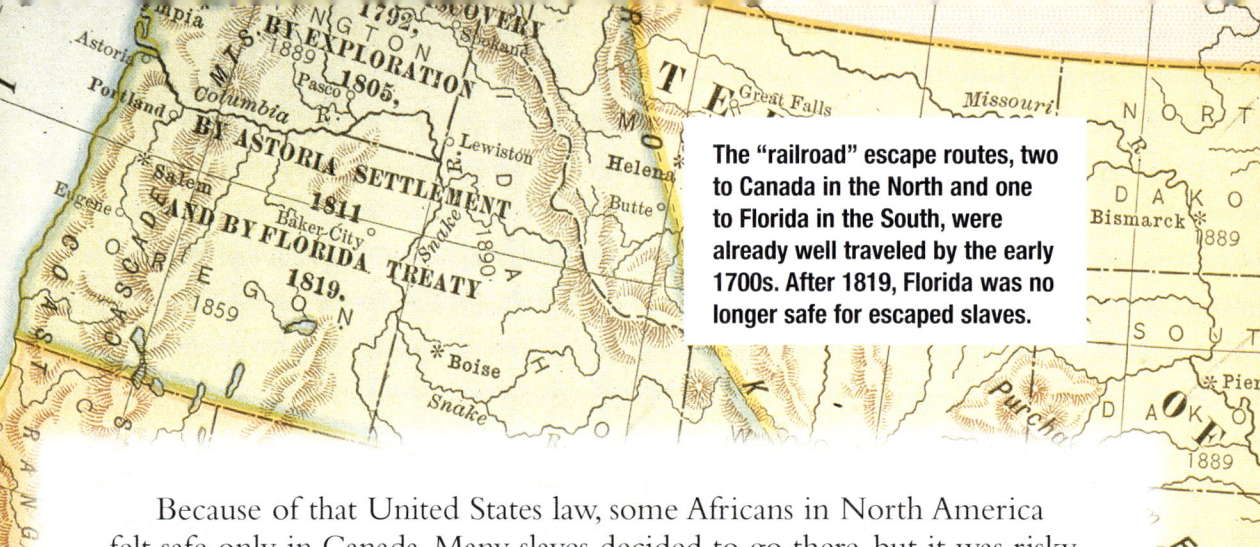

The "railroad" escape routes, two to Canada in the North and one to Florida in the South, were already well traveled by the early 1700s. After 1819, Florida was no longer safe for escaped slaves.

Because of that United States law, some Africans in North America felt safe only in Canada. Many slaves decided to go there, but it was risky. Every step of the way, those escaping slavery had to watch out for slave catchers. Slave catchers got a big reward for every person they captured.

Runaway slaves who got caught could expect punishment. Thousands and thousands of slaves ignored the warning. They decided any risk would be worth taking to escape slavery.

Two Directions

People who took the Underground Railroad used words borrowed from real railroading. The "conductors" were the people who led the way. The "passengers" were the runaways. "Stations" were safe stopping places. "Agents" and "stationmasters" were the people who helped along the way.

The Underground Railroad had no fixed route. Conductors led passengers going north along two general paths. One route headed for the Great Lakes, on the border of the United States and Canada. On the way it passed through Cleveland and Sandusky, both in Ohio. The other route ran northeast through New York and New England.

The passengers met free African Americans and caring white people along the way. These were the abolitionists, who were working to abolish, or end, slavery. To get to the North, the passengers often traveled at night. At several points they had to cross mountains. At times they hid in caves. At other times they hid in farm buildings. Some left the Underground Railroad once they reached Pennsylvania or New York City. There they could blend in with free African Americans. Some could get jobs as sailors on ships docked in the harbors.

ORIGINAL AREA OF THE UNITED STATES 1783
CEDED BY SPAIN 1819
LOUISIANA
GULF OF MEXICO
Lake Superior
L. Michigan
Lake Huron
Lake Erie
L. Ontario
MINNESOTA
WISCONSIN
MICHIGAN
IOWA
MISSOURI
ARKANSAS
LOUISIANA
MISSISSIPPI
ALABAMA
GEORGIA
TENNESSEE
KENTUCKY
OHIO
INDIANA
ILLINOIS
PENNSYLVANIA
NEW YORK
NORTH CAROLINA
SOUTH CAROLINA
FLORIDA
APPALACHIAN MTS.
OTTAWA
Montreal
Toronto
Kingston
Chicago
Detroit
Cleveland
Pittsburg
Philadelphia
Richmond
Norfolk
Raleigh
Columbia
Charleston
Savannah
Atlanta
Nashville
Memphis
Montgomery
Jackson
Vicksburg
Baton Rouge
New Orleans
Mobile
Pensacola
Tallahassee
Jacksonville
St. Augustine
Tampa
Miami
Key West
STRAITS OF FLORIDA
C. Sable
Little Rock
Hot Springs
Fort Smith
Springfield
St. Louis
Jefferson City
Kansas City
Topeka
Des Moines
Madison
Milwaukee
St. Paul
Minneapolis
Duluth
Indianapolis
Lansing
Columbus
Frankfort
Charleston
Wilmington
Cape Fear
Galveston
Houston
Dallas
Scale of Miles
0 50 100 200 300 400

Not all passengers headed north. Some went south to Florida, which in the early 1800s was Spanish territory. The newcomers lived among a tribe of Native Americans, the Seminoles, who welcomed them. But the United States government wasn't happy about that. Florida was like Canada in that U.S. laws didn't apply there. In 1819 Spain sold Florida to the United States. Suddenly Florida was no longer a safe place for former slaves to be.

Why Slavery?

Why was slavery permitted in America? It was allowed for the simple reason that English settlers needed workers on their farms.

When Europeans first sailed to the Americas, they had different ideas about what they wanted there. The Spanish wanted gold. They also thought they had a duty to convert Native Americans to Christianity.

The French were eager to trade. The British had other ideas. They saw America as a big basket of food, tobacco, and various raw materials. The British wanted cotton and flax for making clothes. They wanted the leaves of the indigo plant for making blue dye. They wanted rice and tobacco. The South's warm weather made it a great place to grow those crops. Colonists were eager to grow them on plantations, or huge farms.

The colonists couldn't build and run those plantations without workers. At the time there just weren't enough laborers in the New World.

At first, some colonists made deals with people eager to leave Europe. A colonist paid the cost of a worker's trip to America. In return the newcomer promised to work for the colonist without pay for a number of years. Some Africans made this deal, too.

In the 1850s, a photographer took this picture of Africans working in a field.

An unfinished quilt in the star pattern hangs over a chair.

Plantation owners still couldn't get enough workers this way. They tried to force Native Americans to work for them, but that failed. So they began enslaving Africans. The British wrote laws in favor of slavery. One law said that any child born to an African or African American woman in America could become enslaved. Many Americans understood how wrong slavery was. But they didn't think they had the power to stop it.

The Civil War finally ended all slavery in the United States in 1865. Until then, enslaved people did much of the hard labor in the United States. And most of them dreamed of traveling the Underground Railroad to freedom.

Unraveling a Riddle

One day in 1994, more than 100 years later, a woman named Jacqueline Tobin bought a quilt from Mrs. Williams in the Charleston Market. After Mrs. Tobin took the quilt home to Colorado, she remembered what Mrs. Williams had told her about the Underground Railroad. She went back to see Mrs. Williams, hoping to learn more about patchwork quilts in the days when African Americans were escaping to freedom.

Mrs. Williams came to trust the woman from Colorado and told her a kind of riddle she had learned as a child. Each sentence in the riddle described a pattern sewn into a patchwork quilt:

"There are five square knots on the quilt every two inches apart.

They escaped on the fifth knot on the tenth pattern and went to Ontario, Canada.

The monkey wrench turns the wagon wheel toward Canada on the bear's paw trail to the crossroads.

Once they got to the crossroads, they dug a log cabin on the ground.

Shoofly told them to dress up in cotton and satin bow ties and go to the cathedral church, get married and exchange double wedding rings.

Flying geese stay on the path and follow the stars."

The red outline shows the bear's-paw pattern. It is thought that the color of the paw in a freedom quilt was also used to indicate the escape route.

12

To someone who knew nothing about quilts, Mrs. Williams's statement would have sounded rather strange. But Mrs. Tobin knew some history of quilts. She recognized the names of many quilt patterns, such as Bear's Paw and Log Cabin, in the puzzling words Mrs. Williams told her. Mrs. Tobin suspected they were part of a code. But what did the code mean? And what did it have to do with the Underground Railroad?

Mrs. Williams gave her opinion. When slavery was legal, she explained, everyone, enslaved and free, slept under quilts. When houses were cleaned, quilts were hung outside in the fresh air. To free people this meant only that hard work was underway. But among enslaved people, each pattern had a special meaning.

Quilts, Mrs. Williams said, were like billboards. They announced the time to flee. A monkey-wrench pattern, for example, meant that it was time to gather tools. Tools included objects that would be useful on the trip. A quilt with a wagon-wheel pattern meant something, too. Mrs. Williams remembered what her grandmother had told her. A wagon wheel was a signal to pack up things that a wagon could carry. A quilt whose pieces were sewn together to look like the print of a bear's paw was another secret signal, she said. It told passengers to follow the paths bears took in the woods. Those paths always led to water.

A pattern that looked like a crossroads, Mrs. Williams said, was a code for Cleveland, Ohio. There passengers could board a boat and sail across Lake Erie to Canada. Even the place a quilt was aired had a special meaning. A new quilt aired in a special spot said that a train—a group of passengers—was on schedule. A quilt with a tumbling-block pattern, hung on a fence, meant it was time for passengers to pack up and join the train.

13

Links to Africa

Jacqueline Tobin not only knew a lot about quilts. She also liked to collect the stories of women's lives. She guessed that the use of quilts to send messages wasn't new. How could she find out if her guess was right? She decided to look for an answer where most enslaved people came from—West and Central Africa.

Tobin visited Dr. Raymond Dobard at Howard University. Dobard was both a quilter and a historian. When Tobin told him Mrs. Williams's story, he became very interested. He had always suspected that passengers on the Underground Railroad had used quilts as codes. But he didn't know how.

What he did know a lot about were the many skills Africans brought to America and passed on to their children.

One skill was being able to "talk" without speaking or writing. Dancing, drumming, and singing were part of African religions. Africans also used drumming to send messages across forests and plains.

Another skill was using pictures to "talk." People in Africa had secret societies. Girls and boys learned their groups' secrets when they became adults. To keep others from learning those secrets, each group "talked" using its own symbols, codes, and stories. Another skill Africans brought to America was the ability to make cloth. The patterns on the cloth often told people what groups its makers belonged to.

At a market in Mali, in West Africa, people wear a variety of colorful patterns. Like patterns on the freedom quilts, some of these patterns "talk," too. They may tell where the wearer is from.

Africans were terrific storytellers, too. Each group had an official storyteller called a griot (GREE•oh). Griots used stories to pass a group's history and legends from generation to generation.

Still another skill Africans brought to America from their homeland was blacksmithing–making objects out of hot iron. Such skilled slaves were able to avoid the backbreaking work in the fields. Enslaved Africans often used their skills to survive and to seek freedom.

A Samburu woman blacksmith in northern Kenya, in Africa, forges a piece of metal. This has always been a highly-valued skill.

In 1739, a group of enslaved Africans seeking freedom took up guns against their masters in South Carolina. While marching from plantation to plantation, these slaves played drums, which drew even more slaves to join them. After the uprising was stopped, South Carolina and other colonies quickly outlawed "talking drumming." However, the slaves didn't need drums to communicate. They beat out rhythms on cooking pots. The skill of talking without words continued to serve them well.

The songs enslaved people sang helped them, too. These songs came to be called *spirituals*. To white people, spirituals sounded like Christian hymns. But they were actually coded songs. Canaan was not the Promised Land of the Jews. Canaan was Canada. The song "Steal Away" was not about going to Heaven. It was about escaping to freedom.

TFK DID YOU KNOW

Hearing Freedom's Call

Some conductors on the Underground Railroad were excellent singers. They sang to warn passengers to stay hidden. They sang when it was safe to come out. They used spirituals like "Steal Away" to give tips to people seeking freedom. One verse says:

> My Lord calls me, He calls me by the thunder
>
> Green trees are bending, poor sinner stands a trembling
>
> Tombstones are bursting, poor sinner stands a trembling
>
> My Lord calls me, He calls me by the lightning

You might wonder what the tips are. They're in code. The first line meant that it was smart to leave during a storm. Rain would wash away footprints. It would also wash away any human scent that dogs might follow.

"Green trees are bending" was a reminder that spring was a good time to leave. Slaves often held secret meetings in graveyards. Experts think that the line about tombstones refers to those graveyards.

The meaning of the chorus is easy to understand:

> Steal away, steal away,
> Steal away to Jesus.
> Steal away, steal away,
> I ain't got long to stay here.

A painting shows enslaved Africans dancing.

17

More Puzzles to Solve

What part did quilts play in plantation life? Quilting parties were one of the rare times when enslaved people could enjoy themselves. They made fancy quilts for special occasions. They made sturdy quilts for everyday use.

When making quilts for a plantation owner's house, quilters sewed in regular patterns. They used colors that plantation owners liked. When making their own quilts, enslaved women worked with freer hands. They made their patterns curved or jagged.

Some of the slaves who lived in these little houses on a plantation in South Carolina talked to each other by drumming on pots. Some of them used quilt patterns to communicate.

A log-cabin pattern contains strips of material that look like logs. Their square centers are usually red. African Americans made the centers yellow, black, or dark blue. That meant that their log-cabin pattern stood for a real house, one that welcomed passengers on the Underground Railroad.

Unfortunately, no known freedom quilts still exist. Their original owners often washed them in boiling water, and the soap they used ruined the fibers. So most of the quilts just wore out. Sometimes worn-out quilts got sewn inside new quilts. Sometimes they just got old and were thrown away.

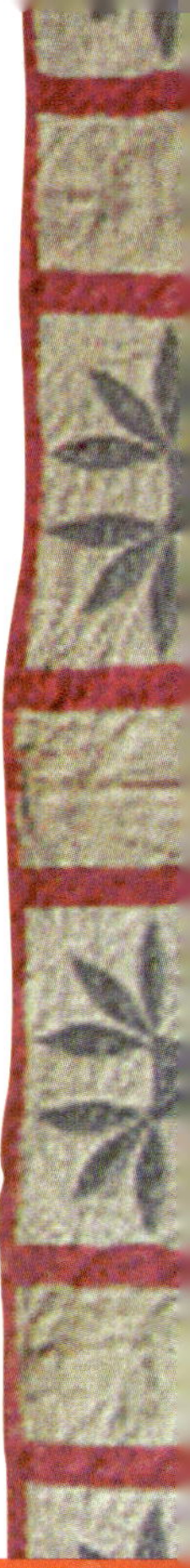

Clues but No Proof

Dr. Dobard believed Mrs. Williams's story about freedom quilts. He had heard rumors about them. Now Jacqueline Tobin had found in Mrs. Williams's stories a missing piece of the puzzle. Dr. Dobard was sure of it. The freedom quilts weren't just the stuff of rumors. They were real!

Quilts that enslaved people made are worth a great deal of money today. Most of them are fancy quilts, made for special occasions. Few of the everyday kind still exist. And no one has come across an original freedom quilt.

TFK DID YOU KNOW

Modern-day quilters follow many of the same patterns used in the freedom quilts, but they have no plan to send secret messages with them. Today's quilters use the designs because they're pretty and they want to carry on the traditions from quilters of long ago.

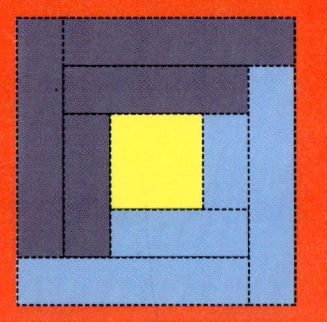

Log-cabin pattern 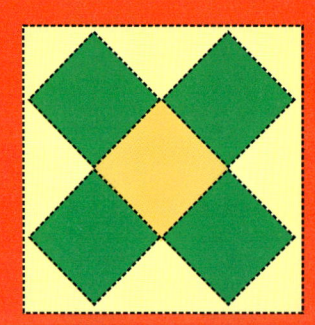   **Crossroads pattern** 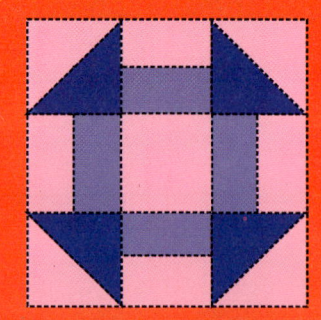   **Monkey-wrench pattern**

This "fancy quilt," with its applique pattern, was made by a slave in Mississippi between 1855 and 1858.

If someone stepped forward with a freedom quilt, it could help explain the strange riddles Mrs. Williams learned as a child. What were the "five square knots on the quilt" that she spoke about? What about the "fifth knot on the tenth pattern"?

Here is Dr. Dobard's explanation. In Africa people sometimes used beads or knotted rope to remind themselves of a certain story or idea. The Luba people of West-Central Africa did something like this. But instead of using knots, they pushed pins and pegged beads into a board called a *lukasa*.

Dr. Dobard thought that a quilt that contained beads or knots might also trigger memories. But they would remain a code, known only to the African Americans who made or used the quilts.

Enslaved Africans escaping to freedom on the Underground Railroad

In 1997 Mrs. Williams told Mrs. Tobin and Dr. Dobard another story about freedom quilts she had memorized as a child. One sentence from the story said, "Men put on coveralls and went fishing on sailboats and came back and ate fish on Dresden plates."

Coveralls? Sailboats? Dresden plates? What could they mean?

Mrs. Tobin and Dr. Dobard believe the story tells what happened after passengers got to the North. They put on coveralls so they would blend in with free black sailors and dockworkers. And the plates? Dresden plates did exist. They were fancy and expensive, and they came from Germany.

But the Dresden in Mrs. Williams's story could mean something else. In Canada passengers settled in several places. One of them was Dawn Settlement, near the city of Dresden. Dresden had many ties to the Underground Railroad. One of its residents was Josiah Henson. The writer Harriet Beecher Stowe used him as the model for Uncle Tom in her novel *Uncle Tom's Cabin*.

By 1998 Mrs. Williams was becoming more and more frail. She wasn't strong enough to get to the Charleston Market. Mrs. Tobin found her at her brother's home. Piles of quilts surrounded her. Mrs. Williams told Tobin to sit and called her "little girl."

Mrs. Williams had no children to carry her knowledge to another generation. Mrs. Tobin felt that Mrs. Williams wanted her to do it. Two weeks later Mrs. Williams died. And Mrs. Tobin wrote a book that keeps alive what Mrs. Williams knew about freedom quilts.

Does the code Mrs. Williams talked about prove that freedom quilts existed? Does it prove that freedom quilts played a part in the Underground Railroad? Maybe. Slaves seem to have made a lot of quilts. However, quilts with codes sewn into them haven't turned up anywhere.

This is the cover of Mrs. Tobin's book.

Harriet Beecher Stowe based the character Uncle Tom on Josiah Henson.

Quilting has been a favorite occupation through the years. It may never again have the importance it had in the days of the Underground Railroad.

But that doesn't mean they never existed. As we have seen, enslaved Americans were experts at sending messages without words. Quilts would have been a super way to do just that.

Clues to the way the Underground Railroad worked grow fainter every year, but it will never be forgotten. Thousands of people made their way to freedom on the Underground Railroad. It seems highly likely that coded quilts, now lost to time, helped point the way.